W9-AHF-556

AMAZING PETS

STICKER ACTIVITY BOOK

Pull out the sticker sheets and keep them by you as you complete each page. There are also lots of extra stickers to use in this book or anywhere you want! Have fun!

NATIONAL GEOGRAPHIC
Washington, D.C.

Consultant: David Alderton
Editorial, Design, and Production by
make believe ideas

Picture credits: pp 1–40: all images Shutterstock except for: **iStock:** 1 tl, 3 tr, 13 tl; **Make Believe Ideas:** 1 tm; ml; m; mr; br (chinchilla), 2 tm, 3 ml (parrot); m; br (hay, apple), 4 tl, 6 tl; ml; m; bl (lettuce); bm (lettuce x3), 7 tm; m; 8 tl; tm; tr; ml; m; mr, 9 mr (red-and-green macaw); bm (Senegal parrot); br (blue-and-yellow macaw on perch), 10 m; mr, 11 tm (jewel); tr; m; br, 12 tm; bl, 13 mr, 14 tm (husky); m (chow chow puppy); bm (leaves x3), 16 bl, 17 m; bm, 18 tl; tm; tr; ml; m; mr; bl; br, 19 tl; tm; tr; ml; m; mr; bl, 20 tl, 21 ml, 22 ml; m; mr (butterflies x4); bl; bm; br, 23 bl; br, 24 m (guinea pigs x2); bl, 25 tm, 26 tm x2; br, 27 br (rabbit), 29 mr (red-and-green macaw); bl (Jenday conure), 30 ml; m, 32 tl; tr; mr, 34 tm (small spiders x4), 35 br, 39 tm; bl; bm; br, 40 ml (guinea pig, rabbit, frog, spider, black puppy); bl; **National Geographic Stock:** 2 tr, 5 tr, 13 br.

Sticker pages: all images Shutterstock except for: **ITF:** 40 fish: orange; **Make Believe Ideas:** 2, 3 spider; rabbits: black-and-white, brown-and-white; apple; lettuce, 4, 5 toys: rainbow ball x3, yellow ball x2, green ball x2, red ball x2, blue ball x2, ball with feathers, mouse; chinchilla; wool: red, blue; guinea pigs, 6, 7 seeds; hay; rabbit: broccoli; sliced fruit: banana x2, kiwi, plum, pear; apple; carrot; carrot slice x3; raspberry x2; peapod; lettuce; blackberry; cherry; strawberry; birds x3, 8, 9 kittens: tortoiseshell, cream, blue-and-cream; all birds except green bl, red-and-blue tm; butterflies: blue x3, pink x3, 10, 11 toy mouse; fur: tortoiseshell, ginger; wool: pink x3, blue x3; kittens: gray (head and paws), black-and-white, 12, 13 mouse; kittens with wool x3, 16, 17 boxer dog; lamb; sheep, 18, 19 hamster x5; sliced fruit: banana x3, plum x2, pear, apple; plum; blackberry x3, 20, 21 all hamsters except hamster ml, hamster on back x2, hamster in house, 22, 23 equipment x11; horses x7, 24, 25 guinea pigs x3; hay; piglet bl; spotted piglet m, 26, 27 rabbits: black-and-white, white; guinea pig, 28, 29 all birds except budgerigar mr, blue-and-yellow macaw bm, 30, 31 shell x6; clownfish; goldfish (all orange) x4, 32, 33 flower x9; turtles x11; lizards x5, 34, 35 bugs x8; all frogs except frog bl, 36, 37 crown; apple; hat x2; boot x2; vest; shovel; tools; fork, 38, 39 leopard gecko; spider; puppy, 40 birds x8; yellow fish; rabbit; guinea pig; frog; black puppy; **National Geographic Stock:** 8, 9 ginger cat, 10, 11 cats: Siamese, Persian, 12, 13 white-and-gray cat, 14, 15 Afghan hound; golden retriever.

Pets come in all shapes and sizes!

tabby cat

ant

chinchilla

Sticker cool pets in the photo frames.

The Chihuahua is the world's smallest dog breed.

Some pets aren't so fluffy!

red-eared slider turtle

Draw your dream pet here!

bicolored rabbit

Sticker the missing rabbits.

Follow the lines to see which rabbit has found the carrot!

Rabbits can hop for short distances at a speed of 50 miles an hour (80 km/h)!

Munch!

Eclectus parrot

Color the hungry horse and sticker her missing snacks.

3

All pets love playtime!

Finish

Rats enjoy playing games with humans, just like cats and dogs.

Help this rat find the way to his friend!

Start

Color the kitten and sticker his toys.

Find and sticker five balls for the puppy.

Draw the other half of the rabbit.

Beep beep!

Who's playing in the grass?

Sticker the Chihuahua peeking out the window, then decorate the caravan.

Syrian hamster

5

Tasty treats for hungry pets!

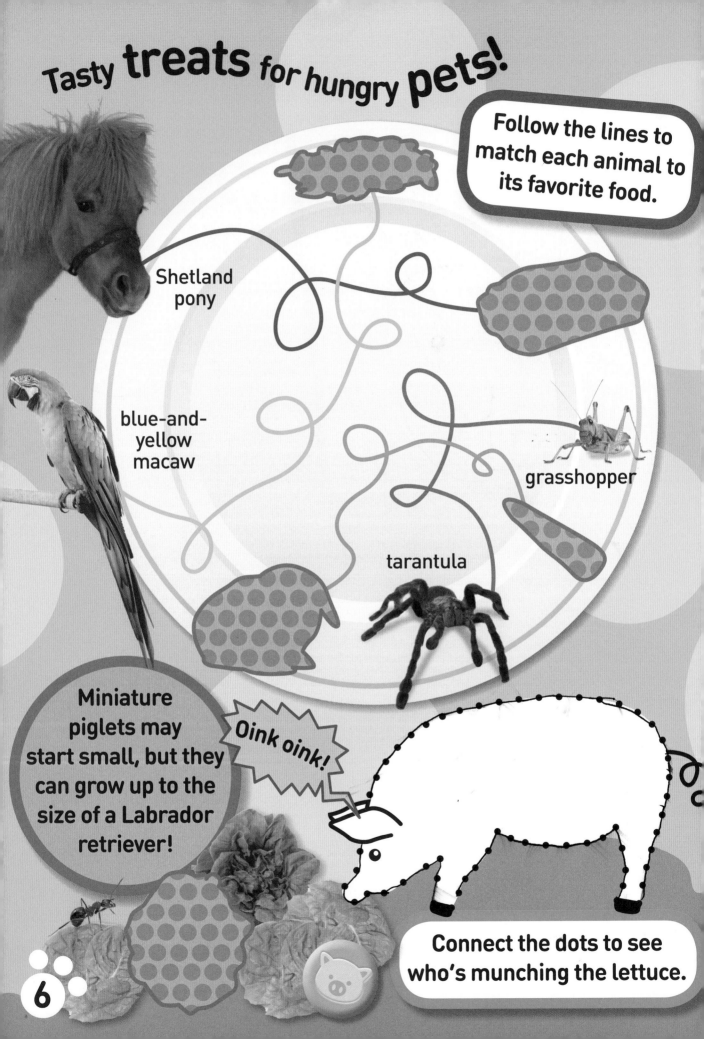

Follow the lines to match each animal to its favorite food.

Shetland pony

blue-and-yellow macaw

grasshopper

tarantula

Miniature piglets may start small, but they can grow up to the size of a Labrador retriever!

Oink oink!

Connect the dots to see who's munching the lettuce.

How many hungry birds can you count?

....

Decorate the pretty puppy's food bowls.

Chloe

Angel

Senegal parrot

shih tzu

I'm hungry!

Hamsters store food in cheek pouches, which can make their heads appear three times bigger!

Sticker what the hamster is eating.

It's **snoozing** time for cute pets!

Sticker the kittens in their baskets.

Cats have an extra eyelid that cleans and protects each of their eyes.

Sticker two sleepy heads.

Draw a kennel for the sleepy puppy.

English cocker spaniel

When a bird sleeps, its legs lock to stop it from falling off its perch.

parakeets

scarlet macaw

Sticker more birds on the branches.

red-and-green macaw

blue-and-yellow macaw

Senegal parrot

Yawn!

Who's sleeping here?

9

There are lots of **amazing** cats!

The ancient Egyptians had pet cats!

Make the royal cats colorful!

Sticker the cat breeds. Hint: The shapes will help!

Scottish fold

Persian

Maine coon

Himalayan

sphynx

Siamese

Devon rex

Russian

Can you get to the ruby at the center of the pyramid?

Meow?

Start

Cats have different patterns on their fur to help them hide!

The Bengal cat is a domestic cat crossed with the Asian leopard cat.

Kitties purr and meow!

MEEW!

What's the kitten scared of?

Cats may roll on their backs to play fight.

Cats can see six times better at night than humans.

Help the cat find his toy in the dark.

There are lots of cool dogs!

Match the moms to their babies.

husky

basset hound

chow chow

Sticker the dog breeds. Hint: The shapes will help!

Afghan hound

golden retriever

border collie

pug

Draw your own dog breed.

Yodel!

The basenji, a dog from Africa, yodels instead of barking.

This beagle puppy has chewed his picture! Can you put it together again?

Scottish terrier

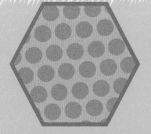

German shepherd

Dalmatian

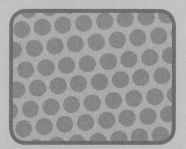

shih tzu

Sticker awards for the fancy pups.

poodle

Chinese crested dog

Pekingese

Have fun with **puppy** training!

Most dogs recognize about 15 commands. One border collie named Betsy can recognize over 340 words!

Lie down

Shake hands

Roll over

Sit

Dogs such as sheepdogs can be trained with whistles!

Sticker a whistle and some sheep for the collie to herd.

Little pets are lots of fun!

Rats laugh in very high, happy squeaks when they play together.

Connect the dots to see what the mice are sniffing!

Sticker hamsters playing.

18

How many rats can you see? ....

Sticker food for the rats to eat!

Draw a cool home for this little gerbil!

Small pet fun and games!

Sticker pets running through the tunnels.

Small mammals use their whiskers to help feel thei way around an area.

What is the hamster running toward?

Stickers for pages 2 and 3

Stickers for pages 4 and 5

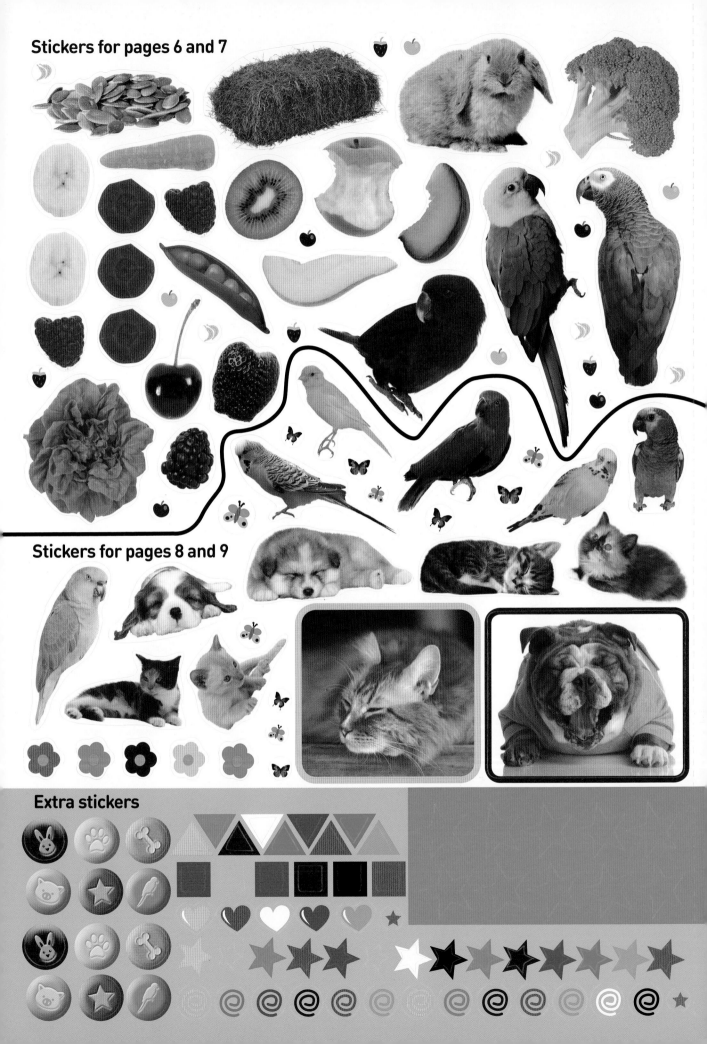

Stickers for pages 6 and 7

Stickers for pages 8 and 9

Extra stickers

Stickers for pages 10 and 11

Stickers for pages 12 and 13

Stickers for pages 14 and 15

Stickers for pages 16 and 17

Extra stickers

Stickers for pages 18 and 19

Stickers for pages 20 and 21

Stickers for pages 22 and 23

Extra stickers

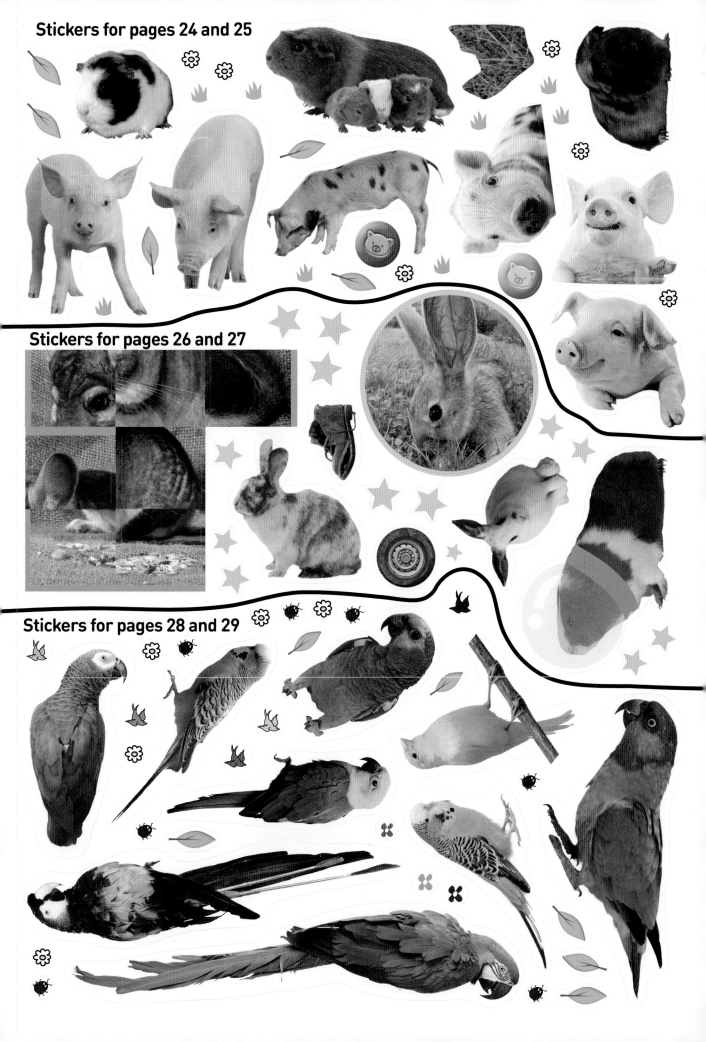

Stickers for pages 24 and 25

Stickers for pages 26 and 27

Stickers for pages 28 and 29

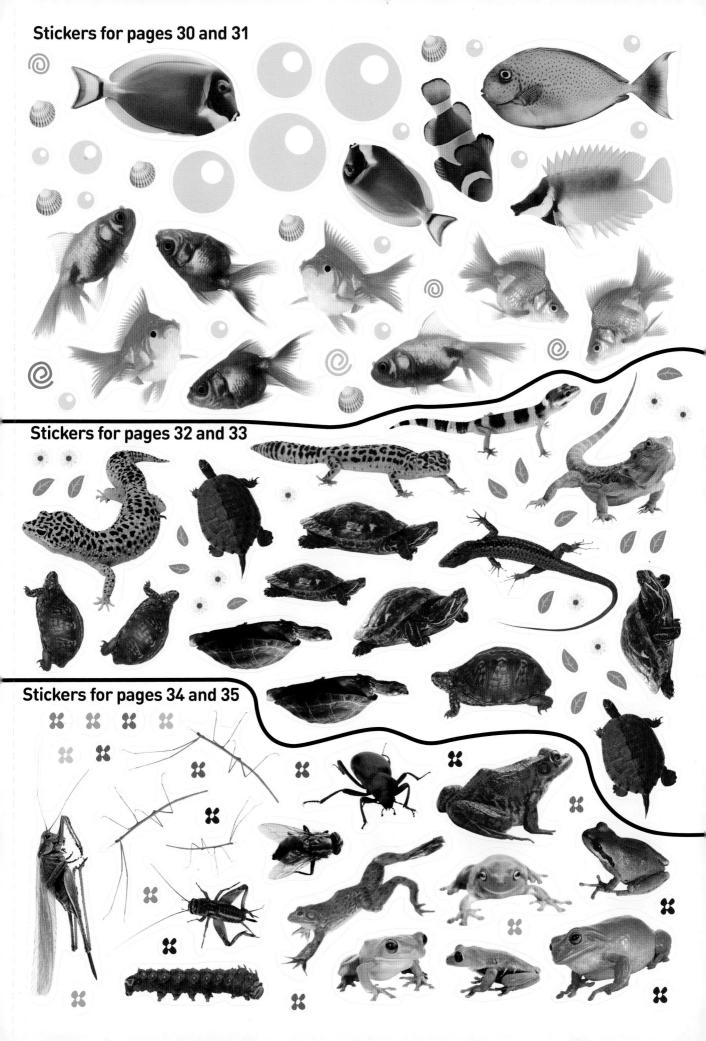

Stickers for pages 30 and 31

Stickers for pages 32 and 33

Stickers for pages 34 and 35

Stickers for pages 36 and 37

Stickers for pages 38 and 39

Stickers for page 40

Extra stickers

Start

Help the hamster find his friend!

Pet hamsters can run up to 8 miles (13 km) per night on a wheel!

Finish

Connect the dots to finish the happy hamster!

Draw a cute pet running on the wheel.

Horses and ponies need love and care!

happy

angry

A horse can show anger or fear by flaring its nostrils and putting its ears back.

Give the horse a colorful mane.

Sticker clothes on the rider.

shire horse

Shetland pony

gypsy vanner

Sticker horses out in the field.

Fill the basket with what you might need to groom a horse.

Guinea pigs and mini pigs love to play!

A happy guinea pig will chatter when it sees its owner.

Draw an awesome hutch for the guinea pig.

Sticker what the guinea pig is eating.

How many pigs are in the pen?

....

Sticker pigs in the teacups!

A guinea pig has traveled into space!

Draw a bunny of your own and give it awesome ears!

Too many carrots, fruits, and sugary treats are bad for rabbits.

Use your stickers to find the chinchilla.

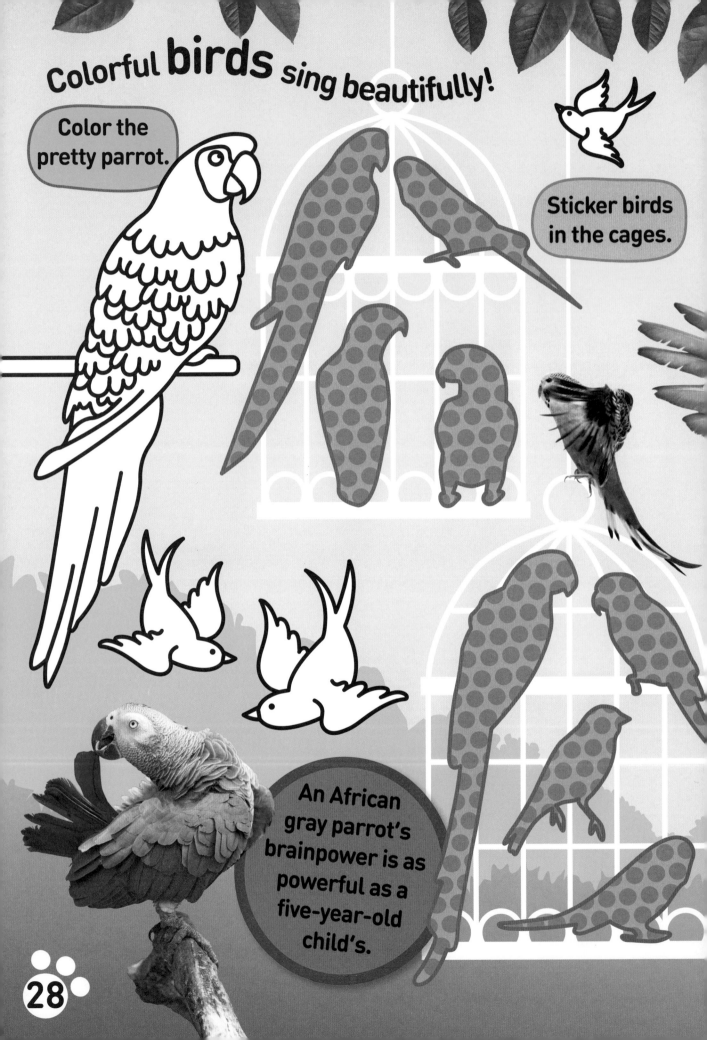

Swim with cool marine fish!

Give these fish beautiful patterns.

clownfish

Desjardin's sailfin tang

Sticker who is playing in the water.

Draw a cool aquarium home for colorful fish!

Fish are covered with smooth scales to help them swim faster.

goldfish

The world's oldest pet goldfish lived for 43 years!

Sticker goldfish in the aquarium.

Wriggly **reptiles** slither and slide!

leopard gecko

A gecko uses its tongue like a windshield wiper for its eyeballs!

bearded dragon skin

ball python skin

leopard gecko skin

Reptiles are cold-blooded, so they use the sun to warm up their bodies.

Sticker the reptiles sunbathing on rocks.

Draw patterns on the snakes.

red-eared slider turtle

Sticker turtles
in the pond.

33

Creepy-**crawly** pets are great!

The Goliath birdeater is a tarantula that eats not just insects, but also frogs and birds!

Can you finish the maze without meeting any spiders?

Finish

Start

Sticker walking sticks!

Copy and color the spider.

34

jumping spider

emperor scorpion

grass spider

Sticker the tarantula's food!

Sticker the frogs on their lily pads.

oriental fire-bellied toad

red-eyed tree frog

Help the red wood ants finish their picture!

Sticker clothes and tools for the worker ants.

An ant can carry 50 times its own body weight. That's like you carrying a car!

At the show!

Who's getting ready in the tent?

Dog shows can include competitions in agility, obedience, flyball, and doggy dancing!

Sticker medals on the winners' table.

Design a trophy!

Which pet won the race?

Finish

Who was best in show?
Sticker the winners!

39

My favorite pets!

Color the frogs!

Sticker birds on the branches.

Finish the pet family photo!

Sticker and draw your favorite fish!

40